Washington, D.C.

★ GREAT ★ CITIES ★ OF THE ★ USA ★

☆ ☆ ☆

LIBRARY OF CONGRESS CATALOGING-IN-PUBLICATION DATA

Loewen, Nancy, 1964-
    Washington, D.C. / by Nancy Loewen.
      p. cm. -- (Great Cities of the United States)
    Includes index.
    Summary: Presents a history of Washington, D.C., from the time it was agreed a capital city should be established, and highlights the activities and attractions in the city.
    ISBN 0-86592-544-5
    1. Washington (D.C.)--Description--1981- --Guide-books--Juvenile literature.
[1. Washington (D.C.)--Description.] I. Title. II. Series.
F192.3.L63 1989
975.3--dc20   89-34085
                                              CIP
                                               AC

© 1989 Rourke Enterprises, Inc.

☆ ☆ ☆

Washington, D.C.

★ GREAT ★ CITIES ★ OF THE ★ USA ★

TEXT BY
NANCY LOEWEN

DESIGN & PRODUCTION BY
MARK E. AHLSTROM
(The Bookworks)

**ROURKE
ENTERPRISES,
INC.**
Vero Beach, FL 32964
U.S.A.

The Capital
of a Nation...

☆ ☆ ☆

TABLE OF CONTENTS

CREDITS

All photos: FPG International

J. Zehrt .... cover photo, 4
David M. Doody 6, 7
Ulf Sjöstedt 10
Peter Gridley 13, 16, 19, 21, 29, 30, 43
Jim Pickerell 14, 35, 40, 41
Icon Communication 15
Jim Howard 17
Kenneth Garrett 20

John Scowen 24, 31
Srenco 25
Martin Rogers 27
David Noble 28
W'Fisiher 33
L & M Photo 34
Michael Mayor 38-39

TYPESETTING AND LAYOUT: THE FINAL WORD
PRINTING: WORZALLA PUBLISHING CO.

☆ ☆ ☆

The Capital of a Nation

It's a typical day in Washington, D.C. Schoolchildren visit the National Archives Building, where they see the original draft of the U.S. Constitution. An older man stands quietly at the Lincoln Memorial, reading the words inscribed in marble. Crouching in front of the black walls of the Vietnam Veterans Memorial, a woman gently traces a name with her finger. On the Mall, friends toss a frisbee around after eating a picnic lunch.

At the same time, there is a bustle of activity on Capitol Hill. Senators and representatives go from one

Visitors view the U.S. Constitution in the National Archives Building.

meeting to another. Their assistants compile research results, write letters and reports, and take phone calls from constituents all across the country. Debates are held, votes taken, decisions made.

This is Washington, D.C., the capital of a nation.

Located on the banks of the Potomac River, Washington was once little more than a muddy rural settlement. But just as early American leaders envisioned a great nation, they also envisioned a great capital city. Today, Washington—with its majestic buildings and sweeping monuments—has fulfilled its promise.

Yet Washington is also a city like all others. It is where people live and work, where they go to school, where they raise their families. The problems of poverty, discrimination, and crime exist here just as they do elsewhere.

In this city of power and leadership, the fight for a better life goes on.

People of all ages enjoy the springtime cherry blossoms along the Mall.

WASHINGTON THEN AND NOW

Establishing a Federal City

During the early years of the U.S. government, no permanent national capital existed. Instead, the capital shifted from cities such as New York, Annapolis, and Philadelphia. By 1783, Congress had decided that enough was enough. What was needed was a "federal city" from which to run the nation. This city would be named Washington, District of Columbia, in honor of first president George Washington and the explorer Christopher Columbus.

Washington, D.C., was named in honor of the first U.S. president, George Washington.

The problem was that no one could agree on where to establish the new city. Everyone thought that the capital would attract a lot of businesses. For that reason, the Northern states wanted the capital in the North. The Southern states argued that the South would be the best place for the capital city. Neither side would give in.

Finally, in 1790, Alexander Hamilton and Thomas Jefferson came up with a plan that everyone could live with. The capital would be located roughly in the middle, but slightly more to the south. For this favor, the South promised to support a certain policy related to Revolutionary War debts.

Congress let President George Washington, a former surveyor, pick the exact site. By January 1791, he had made his choice. The land he chose covered the site of present-day Washington, plus an additional 30 square miles west of the Potomac River. It was located in two states, Maryland and Virginia. President Washington's Mount Vernon home was just 18 miles away.

L'Enfant's Vision

Washington then hired Major Pierre Charles L'Enfant to form a plan for the city. L'Enfant was a French engineer and architect who had fought under Washington in the American Revolution. Assisting him were Andrew Ellicott, who was hired to survey the new federal land, and Benjamin Banneker, a black mathematician and astronomer.

L'Enfant wanted the as-yet-unplanned Capitol Building to be the focal point of the new city. He placed the Capitol and White House on high ground that overlooked the Potomac River. The city's streets were to spread out from the Capitol like rays. Although the area was little more than swamps and pastures at the time, L'Enfant envisioned a grand city of monuments, beautifully landscaped circles, and broad avenues.

Unfortunately, L'Enfant's enthusiasm for the project soon got him into trouble. He paid little attention to such things as budgets or orders from superiors. In 1792 he went ahead and demolished the manor

The cornerstone of the Capitol Building was laid in 1793. Congress first used the building in 1800, before it was finished. It is built of white marble.

house of a rich landowner who had refused to move. President Washington had no choice but to dismiss him. It was Andrew Ellicott who translated L'Enfant's dream into reality.

Construction of the White House—the oldest public building in Washington—was begun in 1792.

The next year, President Washington laid the cornerstone of the Capitol Building. The north wing of this building was finished in 1800, at which point the capital was moved from Philadelphia to its new permanent home. John Adams, who had succeeded Washington in 1797, was the first President to administer the nation from Washington, D.C.

Moving the entire federal government wasn't as difficult as it might seem. The total staff consisted of just 126 people! Still, not everyone was happy with the move. In Philadelphia there had been cultured society and inviting taverns. Here there was nothing—just a few rural settlers and dirt roads that became impassable when it rained. During the first decade of Washington's existence, the area surrounding the Capitol Building contained no more than 20 buildings.

For a time, Congress even debated the idea of moving back to Philadelphia. Then came the war of 1812, and the idea was dropped. Congress had more urgent matters to consider.

The War of 1812

Just three decades after the American Revolution, the United States was fighting the British once again. The main issue was British interference with U.S. shipping, particularly with France. Actually, the whole war could have been avoided. Britain had repealed the laws that had so angered the United States, but in those days before telephone or radio, Congress didn't find out about it until the government had already declared war. By then it was too late.

On August 24, 1814, British troops entered the city after defeating the Americans at the Battle of Bladensburg. The soldiers torched the President's Mansion and the still-unfinished Capitol, along with other public buildings. President James Madison and his wife, Dolley, fled from the town. Somehow, in all the turmoil, Dolley Madison managed to save a famous portrait of George Washington.

The War of 1812 came to an end in early 1815. Reconstruction of the capital began soon afterward. The fire-blackened walls of what was called the President's Mansion were covered with heavy white paint. From then on, the building was referred to as the "White House."

Washington grew slowly in the period between the War of 1812 and the Civil War. An expanding railroad system and the construction of the Chesapeake and Ohio Canal (which connected the Potomac region with the Ohio River) did bring some trade to the area. But Washington did not become the center of commerce Congress had predicted. The young city could hardly compete with such long-established cities as Boston, Philadelphia, Charleston, and New York.

By the 1840's, Washington—with a population of 50,000—covered just a small part of the federal land intended for the city. Congress returned Virginia's portion of the land in 1846.

The Civil War

During the period just before the Civil War, Washington was divided between North and South in both geography and political position. Some people supported the right of the southern states to withdraw from the Union, while others were very much against it. Tension in the city mounted when Abraham Lincoln was elected President. During his inau-guration, military troops stood by to prevent people from rioting.

During the Civil War (1861-1865), Washington's population doubled to 120,000. Many people moved to the city to take official roles in directing the war effort. Troops were stationed to defend the city against Confederate attacks. And freed slaves came to Washington by the thousands, seeking a safe place to live. Businesses sprang up to help take care of the needs of this new population.

In this case, however, it was too much too soon. The city suffered a severe housing shortage. Its public facilities, such as streets and sewer systems, weren't built to handle such use.

After the Civil War came to end, the city directed its attention to a major expansion program. Streets and sidewalks were paved. Sewer lines were installed. Park land was set aside, and hundreds of trees were planted. The city of Washington was finally taking shape.

Washington's Growth

Washington's growth during the Civil War started a pattern that would last for the next hundred years. Although industry failed to bring people into the city, wars and depressions could. In times of crisis, the role of the federal government expanded. This created many new jobs and caused the population to grow.

The next big crisis that caused a population explosion in Washington was World War I. By the end of the war in 1918, Washington had added 100,000 people—up to a total population of 450,000. Shortages affected the city yet again, to be followed by a great building boom in the 1920's.

The entire nation struggled to make ends meet during the Depression years, which began with the stock market crash of 1929. Washington, however, did well during this time. Federal projects to ease the stress of the Depression created thousands of government jobs.

This was soon followed by the increased government activity that resulted from World War II. By 1950, Washington's population hit its all-time high of 800,000. Although the city's population has declined since 1950, growth in the suburbs has been tremendous.

From a hill in Arlington National Cemetery, the grave of Major Pierre L'Enfant overlooks the great city he dreamed of so long ago.

Major L'Enfant designed Washington, D.C., so that the Capitol would be the focal point.

INSIDE WASHINGTON

Washington, D.C., sits on the northeastern banks of the Potomac River, where it joins the Anacostia River. Virginia and Maryland surround the city. Washington covers 68 square miles and has a population of about 626,000. The metropolitan area covers thousands of square miles and has a population of nearly 3.6 million.

Black people make up 70 percent of Washington's population—probably the highest rate in the nation. Of the remaining residents, 41,000 are citizens of other nations, working in foreign embassies or international

Pennsylvania Avenue runs through the downtown area of Washington, D.C.

organizations. This mix of people contributes a great deal to the city's appeal.

Northwest Washington

Washington, D.C., is divided into four unequal sections: Northwest, Northeast, Southwest, and Southeast. At the heart of these sections is Capitol Hill.

Northwest Washington is the section covering the most area. Many of Washington's most important or famous buildings are located here, including the Capitol Building and the White House. Nearly half of the city's population lives in this section. Some of the neighborhoods are poverty-stricken. Others are wealthy or middle-class.

Probably the best-known neighborhood in Northwest Washington—and in all of the city—is Georgetown. Georgetown was a growing tobacco port before Washington was even planned. Its narrow streets and brick

Georgetown is a quiet neighborhood of old homes, many of which were built in the 1700's.

sidewalks speak of a different history from the rest of the city. Many important people live here, some of them in homes that date back to the 1700's. Georgetown is also noted for its many art galleries, bookstores, and boutiques.

The Georgetown community is committed to preserving its heritage. Zoning laws forbid the construction of apartment houses. Construction work or remodeling must conform to the Georgian architectural style.

Along Massachusetts Avenue is an area called "Embassy Row." This is where the ambassadors (official representatives of the countries friendly with the United States) have their homes and offices. Here people can visit the embassies of dozens of countries, including Turkey, Kenya, Korea, Britain, and Japan. One espe-

Georgetown University overlooks the Potomac River.

Events that took place in the Watergate Complex led to the resignation of President Nixon.

cially striking building is the Mosque and Islamic Center, erected by Muslim countries. From the mosque, or public worship place, a slender tower rises 162 feet into the air.

Also in Northwest Washington is the infamous Watergate Complex, which consists of opulent round apartment houses, offices, and a hotel. It was here that the political scandal known as Watergate took place, causing Richard Nixon to resign from the presidency in 1974.

Winding through Northwest Washington is the 1,754-acre Rock Creek Park. People can ride horses, bike, jog, or picnic in this woodland park. Here, too, people can see the remains of a fort built to defend Washington during the Civil War.

D.C.'s Neighborhoods

The Northeast section of Washington is mostly residential. Middle- and low-income neighborhoods house a population that is nearly 90 percent black.

Cutting through the eastern part of this section is the Anacostia River. The National Arboretum and the Kenilworth Aquatic Gardens are found along this river. The arboretum was created during the administration of Theodore Roosevelt (1901-1909). Trees, flowers, shrubs, and other plants line its 415 acres. A special display of dwarf trees, called Bonsai trees, was a gift from Japan in honor of the U.S. Bicentennial.

The Kenilworth Aquatic Gardens is also a peaceful spot to visit. Water plants—including water lilies, lotuses, and hyacinths—grow and bloom out of 44 ponds.

Southeast Washington is another predominantly black section. It has about a fourth of the city's land area and population. The area closest to the Capitol is a wealthy residential area, with many expensive apartments and restored older homes. South of the Anacostia River, however, are many of Washington's most crowded, run-down areas.

The Southwest section of Washington is the smallest in both population and area. Just four percent of the city's people live here. Most of the houses, apartments, and office buildings are fairly modern, the result of an urban renewal project in the 1950's.

Operating in this section of the city are the executive departments of Education, Energy, Health and Human Services, Housing and Urban Development, Transportation, and Agriculture.

The Metro Area

Washington's metropolitan area extends over five counties in Maryland and another five counties in Virginia. It contains suburban cities and towns, as well as areas of farms, hills, and woods. Unlike the city itself, the metropolitan area's population is 78 percent white and just 17 percent black. American Indians, Asians, and other minority groups make up the balance.

Thousands of people living in the suburbs commute to the city for their jobs. Since the 1900's, however, many government agencies and businesses have been established in the suburbs. This means that a greater number of people are able to live closer to their jobs. In Arlington, Virginia, for instance, the U.S. Department of Defense works out of the Pentagon Building. The Pentagon provides jobs for nearly 25,000 people!

More than 25,000 people work in this one building—the Pentagon!

GETTING AROUND

The Washington Area Metropolitan Transit Authority handles public transportation in Washington, D.C. "Metrobuses" are easily identified by their red, white, and blue paint. These days, however, more attention is being paid to the expanding subway system. Called " Metrorail" or simply "the Metro," the subway has 87 stations and extends from the city to the suburbs. Parts of it began operating in 1976. Today the 103-mile transportation system is near completion.

The hub of the Metro system, called Metro Center, is located at

Most people in Washington, D.C., drive to work.

11th and F streets. Its presence has transformed the formerly declining neighborhood into a bustling new shopping district.

Most Washingtonians still depend on their cars to get around. About 70 percent of the people working in the area drive to and from their jobs each day. Expressways have been built to handle the flow of traffic, but Washington still suffers from traffic jams during rush hours.

Three major airports serve the Washington metropolitan area: Washington National Airport, Dulles International Airport, and Baltimore-Washington International Airport. Washington National is one of the nation's busiest. Union Station, located north of the capital, handles passenger trains that connect Washington with other major cities.

The C & O Canal, located in Georgetown, was one of the early transportation systems.

INDUSTRY & TRADE

Not surprisingly, government is the biggest single employer in Washington, D.C. About 374,000 government employees work for the "feds" or for the District of Columbia. These people range from the President and the Supreme Court Justices to thousands of advisors, clerks, secretaries, maintenance workers, and so on.

Washington is also a top spot for tourism. Each year, up to 19 million people trek to the city to take in the many sights. These tourists provide business for scores of hotels, restaurants, and other places. Washington's tourism industry now employs more than 50,000 people and generates $1.5 billion each year.

With the completion of the Washington, D.C., Convention Center in the early 1980's, Washington's reputation as a convention city has grown. The Convention Center has four exhibition halls and can handle the nation's largest conventions. Its 40 meeting rooms can hold anywhere from 100 to 14,000 people. And with more than 50,000 hotel rooms in the metropolitan area, convention-goers have plenty of housing available to them.

Printing and publishing make up the biggest portion of the city's manufacturing. Pamphlets and books covering thousands of subjects are put out by government agencies. Many national magazines are published here as well, including *National Geographic* and *U.S. News & World Report*. *USA Today*, the first successful national newspaper, has its headquarters in Washington. Covering city news are two major newspapers, the *Washington Post* and the *Washington Times*, in addition to many specialty magazines and newspapers.

Washington's role as a leading

communication center extends far beyond printed material. Hundreds of television and radio reporters are quick to inform the world of the U.S. government's activities. And as the center of national government, Washington is also home to many national organizations. These include labor unions, business or professional groups, and nonprofit agencies. Many of these groups send lobbyists to try to influence the government's decisions.

Also attracted by the government are businesses such as accounting firms, research organizations, and finance, real estate, and insurance companies. Law firms, in particular, have flourished in Washington. Many top authorities in specialized fields of law, such as environmental or corporate law, can be found in Washington.

During the 1980's, a change has taken place in Washington's business scene. More and more, the city is attracting national and international firms. Many of these are high-tech companies, dealing with projects such as computer technology and defense communications. In fact, the Washington metropolitan area now has more scientists and engineers than any other city!

Two other notable Washington industries are education and construction. In the metropolitan area are 17 colleges and universities. Many of these, such as George Washington, Georgetown, and Howard Universities, have national reputations. And the construction companies fulfill the housing demand of the ever-increasing suburban population.

Capitol Hill

Many of the nation's most important buildings are located on Capitol Hill. The hill rises 88 feet near the center of Washington and covers about 3.5 acres. "It stands as a pedestal waiting for a monument," reported Pierre L'Enfant back in 1791.

Crowning the hill is the Capitol Building. This is where Congress meets, passing laws and making the decisions that change the course of history. With its massive dome and

The Capitol Building is at the center of Capitol Hill.

tall marble columns, it is probably the most recognized building in the United States. Rising nearly 20 feet from the dome is the bronze Statue of Freedom, modeled after a freed Roman slave.

The Capitol has an interesting history. During the 1790's, a contest was held in which people could submit their designs for the would-be capitol building. The person with the winning design would receive $500—a huge sum in those days—

and a city lot. Unfortunately, Congress was far from impressed with the entries that came in.

Then a man named William Thornton asked for permission to submit a design past the deadline date. Thornton was a physician, painter, and inventor, besides being an amateur architect. His design called for a building of two sections joined by a high-domed center. According to Secretary of State Thomas Jefferson, the proposed building

The Rotunda, which lies under the dome of the Capitol Building, contains many beautiful paintings.

"captivated the eyes and judgment of all." The contest was over.

As it stands today, the Capitol building is 751 feet long and 350 feet wide. From the base of the building to the top of the Statue of Freedom measures 287 feet. The building holds about 540 rooms, many of which are open to the public during tours. Hundreds of paintings, sculptures, and other artwork depict important historical events.

The most breath-taking room in the Capitol Building—the Rotunda—is located beneath the dome. An enormous fresco painting by Italian artist Constantino Brumidi lines the surface under the dome. Fresco is a technique in which special paint is applied to fresh plaster. When the paint and plaster dry, the effect is beautiful.

Brumidi's fresco is called the "Apotheosis of Washington." It portrays scenes from the life of the first president. In order to make the painting seem lifelike from the floor 180 feet below, Brumidi had to make some of the figures in the painting 15 feet high!

The "Apotheosis" was finished in 1865. Brumidi also began a fresco frieze, or sculpted band, around the rotunda, but he died before the work was done. The frieze has since been finished by other artists.

East of the Capitol Building are the three buildings that make up the Library of Congress. The Library of Congress got its start in the early 1800's, when $5,000 was budgeted to stock a library room in the White House. Today the Library of Congress is possibly the largest library in the world. It has more than 85 million items, including books, manuscripts, recordings, and films.

The Supreme Court Building also lies to the east of the Capitol Building. The white marble building was designed by Cass Gilbert and looks like a Greek temple. Here the nine justices of the Supreme Court examine laws and pass down legal decisions that affect the nation. Visitors can watch the sessions, but there is little public seating.

Six congressional office buildings are located on Capitol Hill. Senate offices are found north of the

Like many other government buildings, the Supreme Court Building looks like a Greek temple.

Capitol Building, while the offices of representatives are found to the south. Visitors are welcome to stop by the offices of the officials representing them.

Capitol Hill is also home to the United States Botanic Garden and the Folger Shakespeare Library. The Botanic Garden displays rare plants from around the world. Folger Shakespeare Library contains an important collection of works by and about William Shakespeare, the great English playwright who lived from 1564-1618.

Though only scholars can use its materials, the public is welcome to visit the library. A small theater similar to the playhouses of Shakespeare's time presents Shakespearean and other classic plays. Lectures, concerts, and poetry and fiction readings are also held here.

The Mall

A park area two miles long stretches between the Capitol Building and the Lincoln Memorial. Here, surrounded by stately buildings, people can play softball or frisbee, go on picnics, or ride their bikes. The area is known as the National Mall, or just the Mall. Lining the Mall are many of Washington's most impressive structures.

The Washington Monument is a 555-foot tall obelisk, or pillar, made of white marble. This city landmark honors George Washington. From just about anywhere in the city, people can see its clean white lines sweeping toward the sky. Fifty American flags surround the base.

The Washington Monument is on the Mall between the Capitol Building and the Lincoln Memorial.

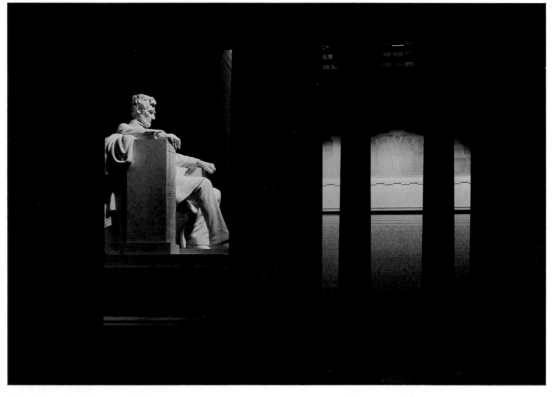

The Lincoln Memorial features an enormous statue of the 16th president.

The monument is hollow inside, with an elevator that runs to an observation room 500 feet high. There are steps inside, too—898 of them! Because of health risks, people are no longer allowed to walk up the steps. They can walk down the steps, however. This way they can read the inscriptions on the blocks of stone, many of which were donated by states or foreign countries.

The Lincoln Memorial stands across the Mall from the Capitol Building. Inside marble walls and columns is Daniel Chester French's statue of Abraham Lincoln, the 16th president who served during the Civil War and put an end to slavery. The 36 columns represent the 36 states that were part of the Union at the time Lincoln was in office.

Carved into the walls are the

words of Lincoln's most famous speeches, the Gettysburg Address and Lincoln's Second Inaugural Address. Inscribed directly above the statue are the words: "In this temple, as in the hearts of the people for whom he saved the Union, the memory of Abraham Lincoln is enshrined forever."

The Reflecting Pool lies between the Washington Monument and the Lincoln Memorial. This long, narrow body of water mirrors the two structures and adds to the beauty of the Mall.

The Thomas Jefferson Memorial is a domed structure surrounded by columns. A bronze statue of Jefferson, the third president, stands in the central room. Thomas Jefferson's most important writings are inscribed on the circular walls. The memorial was dedicated by President Franklin Delano Roosevelt on April 13, 1943.

In front of the Thomas Jefferson Memorial is a shallow body of water

The Jefferson Memorial is reflected in the Tidal Basin.

called the Tidal Basin. The Tidal Basin was a project initiated by First Lady Helen Taft in 1909. In 1912, the mayor of Tokyo, Japan, presented her with 3,000 Japanese cherry trees. These were planted around the Basin. In the springtime the trees bloomed so beautifully that people came to the city just to see them.

Today the Cherry Blossom Festival, held in early April, is an annual tradition in Washington. The festival officially begins when a three-ton stone lantern—another gift from Japan—is lighted by a woman from the Japanese Embassy. The festival draws as many as one million tourists to the capital.

Northeast of the Lincoln Memorial is the Vietnam Veterans Memorial. The memorial is formed by two walls made of black granite, which come together at an angle. On the walls are inscribed the names of all the Americans who died during the Vietnam War, or who are still listed

Many people believe that the simple Vietnam Veterans Memorial is the most dramatic of all the memorials in Washington, D.C.

as being missing in action. The names are listed by date of death. This simple memorial is deeply touching to all who see it.

The Smithsonian Institution—often called the "Nation's Attic"—has its headquarters on the Mall. Nicknamed "the Castle," this red brick building looks like a medieval castle.

Many of the Smithsonian's museums are also located on the Mall. These include the National Museum of African Art, the Arts and Industries Building, the National Air and Space Museum, and the National Museum of Natural History. The National Gallery of Art is also found in this area.

The Smithsonian's National Air and Space Museum may well be the city's most popular tourist attraction. Its grand opening on July 4, 1976, was an important part of the Bicentennial celebration. Here people can see the *Kitty Hawk*, flown by the Wright Brothers in 1903. Charles Lindbergh's *Spirit of St. Louis*, the first plane to fly nonstop across the Atlantic Ocean, is also

exhibited. Spacecraft and rocks from the moon emphasize how quickly flight technology has advanced.

The Smithsonian operates six other facilities in the Washington, D.C., area. The most famous of these is probably the National Zoological Park, more commonly called the Washington Zoo. The zoo's biggest attractions are the two giant pandas given to the United States by the People's Republic of China.

A little more than 100 years ago, no one would have dreamed that the Smithsonian Institution could be so immense. The institution was established at the request of a wealthy British scientist, James Smithson. Though he had never set foot in this country, he willed his fortune to the United States. Smithson's purpose was to found "an establishment for the increase and diffusion of knowledge among men."

Congress was perplexed at first. Nothing quite like that had ever been done before! Finally, in 1846, Congress decided to open a natural history museum. The Smithsonian has been expanding ever since.

The many museums of the Smithsonian Institution display everything you might imagine! The Wright brothers' airplane, the Kitty Hawk, *is located in the National Air and Space Museum.*

Other Attractions

Pennsylvania Avenue is a wide, tree-lined street that runs northwest from Capitol Hill. The avenue is the city's main parade route. It also connects Capitol Hill to the White House, which has a street address of 1600 Pennsylvania Avenue. The White House is set off by beautiful landscaped grounds.

The White House has been the home of all American presidents except George Washington. It has 132 rooms, five of which are open to the public for tours. In the State

Dining Room and the Blue, East, Green, and Red Rooms, people can see historic antiques and presidential portraits. Sometimes a member of the President's family or staff will even stop by to greet visitors.

Many executive office buildings are found along Pennsylvania Avenue. Some of them form what is known as the "Federal Triangle," between the White House and Capitol Hill. The National Archives Building is part of the Triangle. Displayed in the National Archives Building are the Declaration of Independence, the United States Constitution, and the Bill of Rights.

Washington, D.C. has hundreds of other notable places to visit. Ford's Theatre is the playhouse where Abraham Lincoln was shot on April 14, 1865. The theater looks much the same today as it did then.

Arlington National Cemetery holds the gravesites of President John Kennedy and Senator Robert Kennedy, along with the graves of thousands of U.S. soldiers. Near the

Like the Capitol Building, the White House is located on Pennsylvania Avenue. It is the home of the president.

cemetery is the Marine Corps War Memorial, often called the Iwo Jima Statue. The statue depicts the raising of the American flag on the island of Iwo Jima during World War II.

Washington is not only a city of history and politics—it's a city of the arts. World-class concerts, plays, ballets, and operas are performed at the John F. Kennedy Center for the Performing Arts. The Washington Opera, the National Symphony, and other organizations have their permanent residences in the center.

Sports, too, have their place in Washington life. The Washington Redskins football team plays in the Robert F. Kennedy Stadium. The Washington Bullets play basketball in the Capital Center. The Capital Center also houses the Washington Capitals hockey team. Another popular pastime for many Washingtonians is boating on the Potomac River—or enjoying the city's 150 parks.

The John F. Kennedy Center for the Performing Arts is a large complex of theaters and concert halls. It was built after the 34th president was assassinated.

GOVERNING THE PEOPLE

As the only U.S. city that is not part of a state, Washington's city government has an unusual history. For many years, Washingtonians had little say in their own government. This situation has changed in recent years.

The city of Washington was created by and for the federal government. Congress—rather than a state or county—had the authority to govern the city. This power had been granted by the U.S. Constitution.

In 1802, however, Congress decided that a local government should help run the city. Congress appointed a mayor and let voters elect council members. In 1820 voters were allowed to elect the mayor as well. But residents of the District of Columbia still could not vote for representatives in Congress, nor could they vote for the president.

This system was in place for many years. Then, during the period of expansion that followed the Civil War, Congress made some changes. In 1871, the president began appointing the governor and council members. The voters were allowed to elect representatives to an additional council.

Three years later, Washington's city government was turned around yet again. Under the new system, three commissioners were appointed by the president to run the city. The plans of these commissioners were then subject to the approval of the District of Columbia Committees in the Senate and House of Representatives. Washington, D.C., became the only city in the United States whose residents had no political voice.

Following World War II, Washingtonians began expressing dissatisfaction with their voting status. Congress listened and passed the

23rd Amendment to the Constitution in 1964. This gave District of Columbia residents the right to vote in presidential elections. And in 1971, Washington's first elected delegate took office in the House of Representatives. Although this delegate cannot take part in official House votes, he or she may vote in House Committees.

The local level of government soon changed as well. In 1973, for the first time in more than 100 years, Washingtonians were allowed to elect their own officials. Walter E. Washington became the city's first modern mayor in 1974. He was succeeded by Marion S. Barry, Jr., in 1978. Mayor Barry has since been re-elected twice.

In Washington, D.C., the mayor serves a four-year term. Thirteen city council members are also elected for four-year terms. Eight members are elected by voters in eight different election districts, while five members are elected by the city as a whole. The council chairperson is included with the "at large" candidates.

The mayor has the power to veto legislation proposed by the city council. The council, however, can override the veto if there is a two-thirds majority vote.

As in the past, it is Congress who has the final approval over city laws. Congress can make its own laws for the city, or it can overrule laws already passed by the council. The city budget, too, comes under inspection. The budget is first suggested by the mayor and approved by the council. The budget must then be presented to Congress, as well as to the Office of Management and Budget, an executive office of the president.

Even with the recent improvements in their political representation, most Washingtonians are in favor of turning the District of Columbia into a state. That would allow them to elect senators and representatives who would have full voting rights. Legislation to grant statehood to Washington, D.C., is still pending in Congress. If statehood is granted, the District of Columbia would probably become the state of "New Columbia."

The Washington Monument greets the sunrise over the Reflecting Pool.

Though Washington, D.C., is best known for the grandeur accompanying its role as the nation's capital, the city itself faces many of the same problems of other large cities. Crime, poverty, pollution, traffic congestion, and other difficulties present a great challenge to the city.

About 15 percent of Washington's citizens fall below the federal poverty line. An additional four percent of the suburban population is in the same position. Unfortunately, poverty also tends to divide the whites from the blacks. While just three percent of the suburban whites are

More than two-thirds of the residents of Washington, D.C., are black.

Over the years, slums have been cleared to build new office buildings. There is now a shortage of affordable housing.

poor, 14 percent of the blacks in Washington's metropolitan area are poor.

Since anti-segregation laws were passed in the 1950's and '60's, many of the more prosperous blacks have joined the white middle class in moving to the suburbs. Poor inner-city blacks struggle on in what is called "the other Washington."

Since World War II, a slum-clearance program has demolished hun-dreds of decaying row houses in older sections of the city. The houses have been replaced with modern apartment, office, and government buildings. But this effort has not brought relief to the areas that need it most. A lack of good housing for low- and middle-income families is one of the city's major concerns.

Housing costs have risen faster in Washington than in other cities. In 1988, the average price for a single-family home was $132,000. It's not surprising that just 36 percent of Washington families own their own homes—compared to a national rate of 48 percent.

By one estimate, more than 100,000 people in the metropolitan area have to seek help from city- and church-run shelters or soup kitchens. Thousands of these people are homeless.

At the same time, more than 2,400 homes stand vacant. Most of these are too run-down for people to live in them, but could be fixed up for occupation. Many people believe this problem is made worse by an inefficient and possibly corrupt city government.

Recently, Washington has made national news because of its rising homicide, or murder, rate. In 1988, the city averaged four shootings and one homicide per day—one of the highest rates in the nation. So far, the rate in 1989 has been even more disturbing.

Most of these killings are connected to drug dealing. The widespread use of crack, a solid form of cocaine that is highly addictive, is blamed for many of these drug-related shootings. In an attempt to control the situation, the Narcotics Task Force of the Washington Police Department has stepped up arrests. Mayor Barry has also formed "Operation Fight Back," a drug prevention, treatment, and enforcement program. So far, however, these efforts have not turned the trend around.

Still, Mayor Barry insists that the city as a whole remains a safe place for visitors. Most of the homicides have taken place in small, poor sections of the city that tourists are not likely to visit. "Outside of the killings, the city has one of the lowest crime rates in the country," he has said.

Despite its problems, Washington, D.C., remains a powerful symbol of the American people. It proudly presents the best this nation has to offer, even as it points out the areas that still beg for our attention. It remains a city of dreams and leadership. Most of all, it remains a city of hope.

The Iwo Jima Statue, the Capitol Building, and the Washington Monument are powerful symbols of a nation's pride.

*Washington, District of Columbia

IMPORTANT FACTS

- Population: 626,000 (1986 estimate)
  Rank: 16
- Population of metropolitan area: 3,563,000
  Rank: 10
- Mayor: Marion Barry, Jr. (next election, January 1991)
- Capital of the United States

- Land area: 68.25 sq. miles
- Monthly normal temperature:
  January—35.2°F
  July—78.9°F
- Average annual precipitation: 39"
- Latitude: 38° 53' 51" N
- Longitude: 77° 00' 33" W
- Altitude: ranges from sea level to 420 ft.

- Time zone: Eastern

- Annual events:
  Cherry Blossom Festival, April
  Georgetown House Tour, April
  Memorial Day Ceremony, Arlington
   National Cemetery, May
  July 4 Celebration, Capital Hill, July
  Pageant of Peace, December
  New Year's Eve Celebration, December

IMPORTANT DATES

1783—Congress decided to establish "federal city."
1791—George Washington picked site of D.C.
1792-1793—construction of White House and Capitol Building began.
1800—north wing of Capitol Building finished; seat of government moved from Philadelphia to Washington, D.C.
1812-1815—War of 1812.
1814—public buildings torched by British.
1846—slow growth prompted Congress to returned Virginia's portion of federal land.
1861-1865—Civil War.
1865—President Abraham Lincoln shot at Ford's Theatre.
1914-1918—World War I.
1929—stock market crash marked beginning of Great Depression.
1939-1945—World War II.
1950—Washington's population reached all-time high of 800,000.
1964—23rd amendment passed, allowing D.C. residents to vote for President.
1973—D.C. residents allowed to elect city officials.
late 1980's—Increase in drug-related killings and shootings became serious concern.

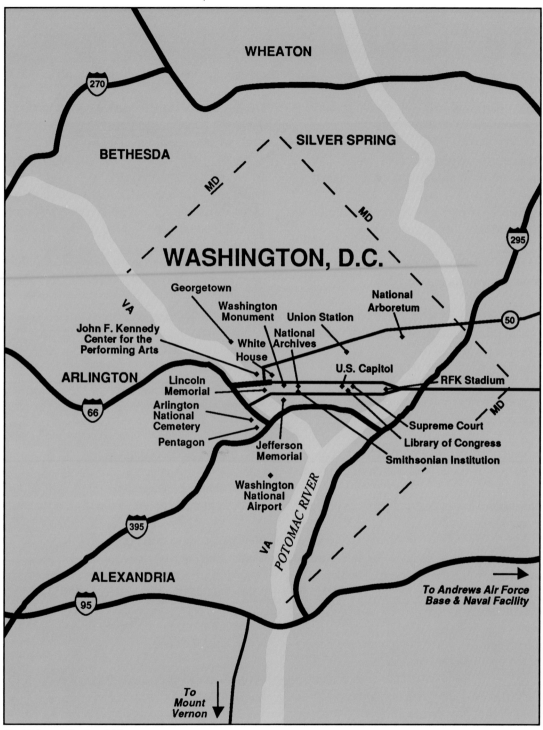

WHEATON

270

SILVER SPRING

BETHESDA

MD

MD

WASHINGTON, D.C.

Georgetown

295

Washington
Monument

Union Station

National
Arboretum

VA

50

John F. Kennedy
Center for the
Performing Arts

White
House

National
Archives

ARLINGTON

Lincoln
Memorial

U.S. Capitol

RFK Stadium

66

Arlington
National
Cemetery

MD

Pentagon

Supreme Court

Jefferson
Memorial

Library of Congress

Smithsonian Institution

Washington
National
Airport

POTOMAC RIVER

395

VA

ALEXANDRIA

To Andrews Air Force
Base & Naval Facility

95

To
Mount
Vernon

©1989 Mark E. Ahlstrom

★ GLOSSARY ★

amendment—an official change to the U.S. Constitution.

arboretum—a place where plants are grown for scientific study or educational purposes.

architect—a person who designs buildings and overlooks their construction.

archives—a place where important documents or public records are stored.

Bill of Rights—the first 10 amendments to the Constitution, guaranteeing personal freedoms.

botanic—relating to the study of plants.

capital—a city in which the government of a state or nation is located.

capitol—the building or buildings occupied by state or national governments.

commissioner—a person in charge of a government department.

Congress—The legislative, or law-making, branch of the U.S. government. The U.S. Congress is made up of the Senate and the House of Representatives.

constituent—a voter; someone who is represented by an elected official.

Constitution—the laws that are used to define the U.S. government.

Declaration of Independence—the document declaring American independence from England, written mainly by Thomas Jefferson in 1776.

embassy—the home and offices of an ambassador, or political representative, who is from a foreign country.

executive—the branch of government that manages and directs the affairs of a city, state, or nation.

federal—having to do with the central government of the United States.

inscription—words that are carved into a hard surface. Can also mean a written dedication.

lobbyist—a person who tries to influence government decisions.

monument—a statue, building, or other marker put up in honor of a person or event.

obelisk—a four-sided pillar that tapers to a point.

rotunda—a large room covered with a dome.

Supreme Court—the highest-ranking court in the United States.

veto—the power of a government official to refuse to sign a bill into law.

INDEX